Roger Hurn

Rising Stars UK Ltd.
22 Grafton Street, London W1S 4EX
www.risingstars-uk.com

NASEN House, 4/5 Amber Business Village, Amber Close, Amington,
Tamworth, Staffordshire B77 4RP

Every effort has been made to trace copyright holders and obtain their permission for the use of copyright materials. The publisher will gladly receive information enabling them to rectify any error or omission in subsequent editions.

All facts are correct at time of going to press.

The right of Roger Hurn to be identified as the author of this work has been asserted by him in accordance with the Copyright, Design and Patents Act 1988.

Published 2008

Text, design and layout © Rising Stars UK Ltd.
Series Consultant: Lorraine Petersen
Cover design: Neil Straker Creative
Cover Image: D.C. Thomson & Co., Ltd
Design: Geoff Rayner, Bag of Badgers
Editorial: Frances Ridley
Illustrations: Bill Greenhead
Photographs:
Alamy: 42, 46
DC Thompson & Co., Ltd: 4, 8, 10, 11, 12-13, 14, 16, 20, 23, 25, 27, 28-29, 30, 34-35
Egmont UK Ltd: 39, 40
Getty Images: 38, 41
VinMag Archives: 11, 18, 19, 24, 36, 42, 44, 45, 47

British Library Cataloguing in Publication Data.
A CIP record for this book is available from the British Library.

ISBN: 978-1-84680-444-1

Printed by: Craftprint International Ltd, Singapore

The publisher would like to thank the following for use of their copyrighted materials:
DC Thompson images © D.C. Thomson & Co., Ltd, 2008. With special thanks to Bill Moodie.
Roy of the Rovers © Egmont UK Ltd, 2008

CONTENTS

COMICS: THE BIG PICTURE

The first comics appeared in Victorian times and they are still popular today. Comics have great characters. They are full of heroes, villains and mischief-making kids!

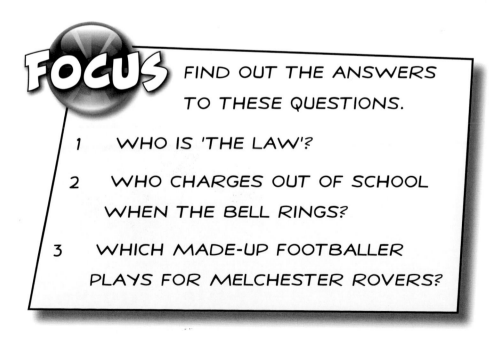

FOCUS FIND OUT THE ANSWERS TO THESE QUESTIONS.

1   WHO IS 'THE LAW'?

2   WHO CHARGES OUT OF SCHOOL WHEN THE BELL RINGS?

3   WHICH MADE-UP FOOTBALLER PLAYS FOR MELCHESTER ROVERS?

ZOOMING IN...

Dan Dare and Judge Dredd

Laying down the Law.

Roy of the Rovers

This guy's on the ball!

Triple Trouble

Watch out! The kids are about!

The Dandy
A comic that
moves with the times.

Desperate Dan
The craziest cowboy in comics.

Roger the Dodger
The king of the dodgy dodge!

The
Bash Street Kids
Too cool for school.

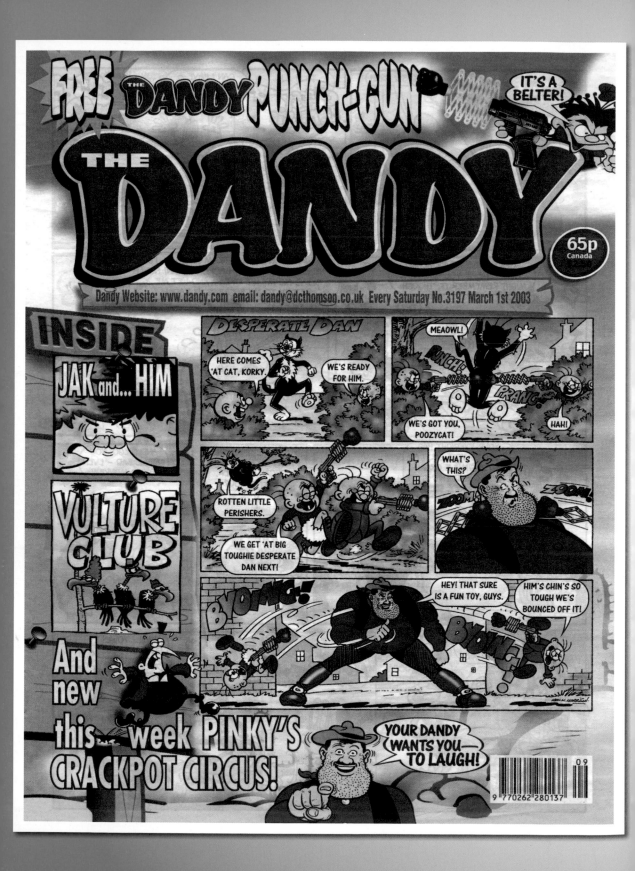

IT'S JUST DANDY

THE DANDY STARTED IN 1937. IT WAS THE FIRST COMIC TO USE SPEECH BUBBLES. IN THOSE DAYS, IT COST TWO **OLD PENNIES**.

YOU CAN STILL BUY THE DANDY TODAY. IT COSTS A LOT MORE THAN TWO OLD PENNIES BUT IT'S STILL FULL OF WILD AND WHACKY CHARACTERS.

THE DANDY WHO'S WHO

Korky the cat

Korky the cat was on the first cover of *The Dandy*.

Korky was always getting up to mischief.

Korky finally retired from *The Dandy* after 70 years!

The Amazing Mr X

The Amazing Mr X was the UK's first superhero!

Mr X fought the **Nazis** during World War Two.

He wore black trousers and a mask, and a white top with a red 'X' on it.

Eric (Bananaman!)

Eric is *The Dandy's* most popular superhero.

He's an ordinary school boy – until he eats a banana.

Then he turns into Bananaman – the world's stupidest superhero!

Ollie Fliptrick

Ollie is a crazy, spiky-haired skateboarder.

His skateboarder buddies are Doug, Smudger and Anna.

Ollie has his own fan club: Ollie Fliptrick's Dandy Club.

THE DANDY LIVES ON!

The Dandy is over 70 years old and is the world's longest running comic.

A few years ago, the comic got a makeover. Now it's *The Dandy Xtreme*. It's fresher, brighter and wilder than ever. Comic fans love it!

> HEY, I'M JAK, DANDY XTREME'S TOP SKATEBOARDING DUDE. I'M MORE POPULAR THAN YOU.

NO WAY! KIDS LOVE ME THE BEST. I'M DESPERATE DAN AND I PUT THE 'WILD' INTO THE WILD WEST!

COMIC FACT

IN 1951, ONE ISSUE OF THE DANDY SOLD OVER TWO MILLION COPIES!

THE WORLD'S STRONGEST MAN

DESPERATE DAN IS A ROUGH, TOUGH COWBOY.

HE FIRST RODE INTO THE DANDY IN 1937
AND HE'S STILL GOING STRONG!

HE CAN CHEW IRON AND SPIT RUST BUT
HIS FAVOURITE FOOD IS COW PIE!

COW PIE RECIPE

Follow this recipe for a belly-busting meal.
Feeds one rooting, tooting, six-gun-shooting cowboy!

HORNS

COW-PIE

TAIL

PIE CRUST – MAKES A WICKED FRISBEE

PIE TIN – MAKES A GREAT CRASH HELMET!

RECIPE

1 cow

10 buckets of extra thick gravy

A sack of flour

50 litres of water

A crane, a cement mixer and

a **flame-thrower**

WHAT TO DO

1. Use the crane to put the cow in the pie dish.

2. Add the extra thick gravy.

3. Put the flour and water into the cement mixer to make the pastry.

4. Shovel the pastry on top of the dish.

5. Make holes in the crust for the horns and tail.

6. Use a flame-thrower to cook the pie.

7. Enjoy!

⚠️ WARNING!

YOU WILL NEED STEEL-CAPPED TEETH TO EAT THIS PIE!

THE TOUGH GUYS' TOUGH GUY

Desperate Dan is the world's strongest man. He can bend lamp posts and lift a cow with one hand. Dan's so hard he even shaves with a blow torch!

Dan lives in the town of Cactusville. He has a pet dog called Dawg – the hardest hound around!

Dan isn't always on the right side of the law. Sometimes he helps other people and sometimes he just helps himself.

DUCKING AND DIVING

ROGER THE DODGER IS A BAD BOY FROM THE BEANO. HE'S BEEN IN THE COMIC FOR OVER 50 YEARS AND IS STILL POPULAR WITH READERS.

ROGER'S MAIN AIM IN LIFE IS TO DUCK OUT OF DOING ANY WORK – ESPECIALLY HOMEWORK! HE'S ALWAYS GOT A TRICKY **DODGE** TO HELP HIM.

Roger the Dodger's Top Dodges Book

The 'Get Out of Going Shopping' Dodge

1. 'Borrow' a red lipstick from your mum.

2. Draw big spots on your face.

3. Tell your mum you can't wait to go shopping.

4. Act surprised when she stares at your face and screams!

5. Make a big fuss when she tells you to stay at home.

6. Settle down and watch TV while she's shopping!

The 'Get Out of Digging the Garden' Dodge

1. Draw a map of your garden with crosses all over it.

2. Tell your mates that a jewel thief used to live in your house – and this map shows where he hid his loot!

3. Relax while your mates dig the garden looking for jewels.

BODGED DODGE

Roger thinks he's really smart but his dodges always backfire – no matter how clever they are. So Roger always ends up in big trouble!

In one story, Roger goes to a party. He's greedy and wants all the food for himself. So he scares off the other kids with a fake scary dog. Then he tucks into the grub. The other kids find out how he has tricked them so they set a real scary dog on Roger!

CLOSE UP:
SCHOOL DAZE

In 1954, the Beano began a comic strip called 'When the Bell Rings'. Its creator was Leo Baxendale. Baxendale said the characters were like 'a herd of **stampeding bison**'.

DAVID SUTHERLAND TOOK OVER FROM LEO BAXENDALE
IN 1962. HE DREW THE KIDS IN FULL COLOUR.

COMIC STRIP FANS LOVE TROUBLEMAKERS. THE BEANO AND THE DANDY ARE HOME TO A WHOLE BUNCH OF WILD KIDS.

THE KING OF THEM ALL IS DENNIS THE MENACE, THE WORLD'S NAUGHTIEST BOY. DENNIS IS A TROUBLE MAGNET – AT HOME, IN THE PARK, AND AT SCHOOL!

SCHOOL REPORT

Name:
    Dennis the Menace

Subject:
    Maths

Teacher's comment:
    Dennis is a Know-it-all! I asked
    him how many seconds there are in
    a year and he said 12.
    January 2nd, February 2nd ...!!!

Subject:
    English

Teacher's comment:
    Dennis loves making up stories
    (about why he hasn't done
    his homework!)

Subject:
   Science

Teacher's comment:
   Dennis likes chemistry – he blew
   up the science lab last week.

Subject:
   Geography

Teacher's comment:
   Dennis is hopeless – he thinks the
   people who live in Moscow are
   called Mosquitoes.

General comment:
   Dennis thinks he's clever because
   he's got an answer for everything!

TROUBLEMAKERS!

Dennis the Menace has been *The Beano's* star mischief-maker since 1951.

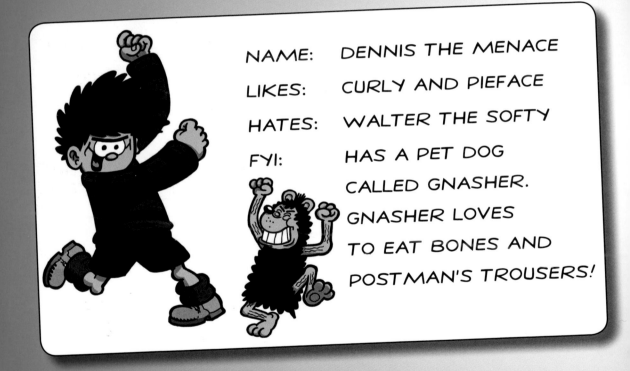

NAME: DENNIS THE MENACE

LIKES: CURLY AND PIEFACE

HATES: WALTER THE SOFTY

FYI: HAS A PET DOG CALLED GNASHER. GNASHER LOVES TO EAT BONES AND POSTMAN'S TROUSERS!

These two girls have been making mischief since 1953.

NAME: MINNIE THE MINX

LIKES: STRIPY RED AND BLACK JUMPERS

HATES: PEOPLE WHO CALL HER 'GINGER'. HER HAIR'S RED – OK!

FYI: FIRST APPEARED IN THE BEANO

NAME: BERYL THE PERIL

LIKES: HAVING THE LAST LAUGH

HATES: PEOPLE TUGGING HER PIG TAILS

FYI: FIRST APPEARED IN THE TOPPER

MORE THAN A GAME

ROY RACE WAS THE FIRST COMIC STRIP SOCCER STAR. HIS ADVENTURES BEGAN IN THE TIGER IN 1954.

ROY'S TEAM WAS **MELCHESTER ROVERS.** EVERY WEEK, THE ROVERS NEEDED ROY'S SKILLS TO SAVE THEM FROM DEFEAT.

Roy Races to Shock Cup Win

Report by Ivor Ball   Picture by Owen Gole

Star Striker on form at the FA Cup semi final.

Melchester Rovers looked down and out in yesterday's FA Cup semi-final. Nottso Athletic were 3–0 up. Rover's die-hard fans were stunned. Was there any way back for their heroes?

There was! Super sub Roy Race came on. He tricked his way past three defenders. Then he lashed the ball into the top corner of the net. Rovers were back in the game!

Next, Rovers won a corner. Roy leaped into the air and headed the ball into the back of the net. Now it was 3–2. Time was running out. Then Roy scored with a cheeky back heel! Rovers were level. But which team was going to Wembley?

No contest! Roy smashed home the winning goal in extra time!

'I'm over the moon,' said Roy. 'It's the magic of the FA Cup!'

Player Profile: Roy Race

Name:
Roy Race

Height:
1m 88cm

Weight:
82kgs

Nickname:
'Racey'

Best moment:
Playing for England

Worst moment:
Rovers getting relegated
in 1981

Main ambition:
For Melchester Rovers to win
the Champion's league.

Roy of the Rovers © Egmont UK Limited 2008

The *Roy of the Rovers* comic ended in 1993.

In the last story, Roy lost his foot in a helicopter crash. He never played again but his legend lives on!

TV COMMENTATORS OFTEN SAY 'IT'S JUST LIKE ROY OF THE ROVERS!' WHEN A PLAYER OR TEAM DOES SOMETHING AMAZING.

FUTURE SHOCK

DAN DARE AND JUDGE DREDD ARE COMIC-BOOK HEROES. THEIR ADVENTURES ARE SET IN THE FUTURE.

DAN DARE MADE HIS FIRST SPACE FLIGHT IN THE EAGLE IN 1950. JUDGE DREDD FIRST APPEARED IN THE COMIC 2000 AD IN 1977. BOTH MEN FIGHT EVIL – BUT THEY DO IT IN VERY DIFFERENT WAYS.

DAN DARE.

Statement:

I believe that we must never use evil to fight evil.

I believe that everybody has the right to a fair trial — no matter what they've done.

I believe that nobody is above the law — not even the law-makers.

JUDGE DREDD.

Statement:

I fight evil by doing whatever it takes. I am the judge, jury and **executioner.** *I zap evil creeps because I am the law.*

DARE TO DREDD

Dan Dare was popular in the 1950s. The stories were set in Earth's **solar system**. Dan Dare's worst enemy was an evil **alien** called The Mekon. Dan Dare was always fair and played by the rules.

DAN DARE FACT

EACH DAN DARE STORY HAD AMAZING FULL-COLOUR ART WORK.

THE ARTISTS USED MODEL SPACESHIPS AND MODELS IN COSTUMES.

Judge Dredd is a popular hero today. In the stories, he fights crime in Mega-City One. His enemies are people who break the law. Judge Dredd makes other people follow the rules – but he doesn't always follow them himself.

GLOSSARY

Alien
A being from another planet.
The Mekon is an alien from Venus.

Stampeding Bison
A charging herd of large shaggy animals with sharp horns and huge heads.

Dodge
A clever trick.

Executioner
A person who kills convicted criminals.

Flame-thrower
A machine that shoots flame from a tube.

Melchester Rovers
A made-up football team based on Manchester United.

Nazis
The Nazi party ruled Germany during World War Two. The Nazis were cruel to many groups of people.

Old pennies
Coins used before 1971. An old penny was worth over twice as much as a modern penny.

Solar System
The Sun and the planets that travel around it.

INDEX